Trial by Fire: Lessons in IT Leadership

Adam Luck

Trial by Fire: Lessons in IT Leadership

Adam Luck

ISBN 9798594710528

© 2020 - 2021 Adam Luck

I dedicate this book to...

- *My parents, who taught me the importance of family, community and Cleveland Indians baseball*
- *My wife, who is my rock and supports me every day*
- *My coworkers, past and present, who inspired these stories*

Contents

Introduction 1

Show up 3

Have empathy 5

Celebrate success 7

Go with your gut 9

Don't leave people waiting 13

Keep perspective 15

Just do it 17

Get back on the horse 21

Give praise in public 23

Don't lose data 25

Follow the money 27

Keep digging 31

Create alignment 33

CONTENTS

Tell the truth 35

Find a process that works 39

Plan for the worst 43

No surprises 45

Scratch and dent the car 47

Fail fast 51

Tell a good story 55

Monitor perception 59

Push your own car 63

Remove bottlenecks 65

Eat your own dog food 67

Encourage innovation 69

Use situational leadership 73

Find the opportunity 75

Create a vision 77

Build a network 79

Don't take it personally 81

Keep improving 83

Don't walk past a mistake 85

Learn to budget 87

Extend your team	89
Do the right thing	93
Measure it	95
Find a cause	99
Learn by observation	103
If you want applause, join the circus	107
Turn friends into family	109
If it hurts, do it more often	111
Ask the right questions	113
Focus on your industry	115
Recognize others	117
Do the dirty work	119
You break it, you buy it	121
Know when to move on	123
Play chess, not checkers	125
Be a duck	127
Summary	129
About the author	133

Introduction

I found myself thinking about my Grandpa Don during the COVID-19 quarantine.

Grandpa Don joined the U.S. Navy in 1942 and became a commissioned officer on the destroyer USS Welles. Between August 1944 and August 1945, the Welles provided support in the battles of Iwo Jima and Okinawa. Grandpa Don was in the opening assault at Leyte Gulf, considered to be the largest naval battle of World War II in the Pacific.

Grandpa Don practiced law before shifting to a career in the retail industry. He was the owner and president of Werner-Hilton, a men's clothing chain founded in St. Louis in 1919 by his father-in-law, Julius Werner. The last of the chain of five stores closed in 1984.

He truly reinvented himself in retirement. Grandpa Don painted, sketched, wrote poetry, and even self-published a few poetry books. You won't find these poems at any bookstore because each edition was created by hand. He wrote, designed, printed, and trimmed each page in the spare bedroom of his condo. He never intended to make a dime. He just loved to create.

When I joined a rock band in high school, Grandpa Don became our biggest (and likely only) fan. He designed our promotional fliers and paid for us to record a demo in a professional studio. Looking back, I think he just wanted to encourage my creative side.

Inspired by his creativity, I wrote a few blog posts about things

I learned while working in the technology industry. I tried to tie each story back to a specific individual as a way of thanking them for their support and the lessons I learned along the way.

I eventually wrote enough of these blogs that I decided to self-publish a book. This book is a collection of stories I've captured over my 10 years as an IT leader. My hope is that you can turn to any chapter for a quick, yet comprehensive leadership lesson. I look forward to receiving my first copy and placing it alongside one of my grandpa's handcrafted poetry books.

Thanks for reading and hope you enjoy.

Adam

Show up

One evening at 10:30 PM, I received a phone call from a colleague. Before I even answered the phone, I knew that they were calling to share bad news. My coworker started the call by asking if I was sitting down. I braced myself for the worst. Our file server experienced corruption, and we lost access to the data.

We had already identified this system as a risk to the organization. We knew about the system's fragility and were working to improve its reliability and redundancy. We knew that any issue affecting this system would bring our company's productivity to a halt. In short, this was as bad as it gets.

I arrived at the office at around 11 PM. I made a few phone calls and notified the IT department of the issue via email. By 11:30, I saw a familiar face, it was our Application Development Manager, Brian! He had a bag filled with energy drinks and candy. Brian pulled up a chair to my desk and made it clear that he was here to support us in any way he could. He wasn't going to leave until we did.

By 1 AM, I saw **another** familiar face. Another Application Development Manager, Robert, arrived with a bag filled with candy and energy drinks. He also told us that he was in it for the long haul. Both Robert and Brian served on different teams within IT. The problems we encountered weren't directly theirs to solve. It would have been sufficient if they offered us positive vibes from their homes.

They both stayed with us throughout the night. They offered guidance, support, and encouragement. Their actions minimized the impact of the issue and helped ensure the completion of some of our critical business processes. Even as the sun rose and the reality of the situation set in, they maintained their positive attitudes and offered continued support.

Before this outage, I honestly don't know if I would have followed their actions under similar circumstances. So many times throughout the day we see opportunities to help and support others, but let those opportunities pass. These colleagues have inspired me to be not just a better coworker, but a better person. I may not be able to pay them back, but I will absolutely try to pay it forward.

Have empathy

I was working as a technology support analyst when I started my day with a strange phone call. I hadn't even unpacked my things yet. The caller, one of my coworkers, was frantic and needed my help. She could not find a file they had been working on.

Our conversation didn't start off too well. I started walking her through some basic troubleshooting steps. She grew impatient as I tried to resolve the issue. Her attitude added to the stress that I was already under as I tried to find the missing file.

I decided to walk up to her office. I ended up restoring the file from a backup a few minutes after I arrived. She cried tears of joy and gave me a big hug. I realized later that day that this interaction left a giant makeup stain on my white shirt.

It turns out she had been working all weekend on that file for a big presentation scheduled later that day with a potential client. I knew it was important that I find the missing data, but I didn't grasp the context until then.

I learned a lot that day. I hadn't considered the concept of the butterfly effect before. Something as insignificant as restoring a file for someone was actually a big deal. I realized that I needed to learn to put myself into other people's shoes.

Just a few weeks later, I encountered another tech support issue that tested my patience. A coworker's computer wasn't turning on. She was angry and didn't bother to hide it. I asked her to check the cable connections below her desk. She informed me they couldn't see the cords because her power was out. She thought her surge protector would keep the computer running.

If this happened just a few weeks prior, I might have mocked my coworker for her lack of knowledge. I realized that I needed to have empathy for her situation. I took a deep breath and walked her through why their computer wouldn't turn back on.

During our chat, I learned a lot about my colleague. She had recently joined the organization and were was working remotely for the first time after decades of serving as an RN in a hospital. I realized that she had every right to be stressed. I needed to walk a mile in their shoes.

While on the phone, her power came back on and we both rejoiced in unison.

Celebrate success

I graduated from Ohio University (OU) in the summer of 2008, which was just a few months after the collapse of Lehman Brothers. Despite having a degree in the in-demand field of technology, I had trouble finding full-time employment. After applying for hundreds of jobs, a medical care management company hired me as a technology support analyst.

I had a tough start at this job. Even though I had a degree, I was unprepared for the workforce and lacked some key technical skills needed for my entry-level position. Since I wasn't contributing much to the team, I struggled to establish meaningful relationships with my peers. I had no confidence and wondered if I had a future in technology.

I tried to make up for my lack of experience by having a strong work ethic and a positive attitude. I leveraged the customer service skills and patience gained while working for my family's retail store in high school. I may not have been the fastest to find a solution, but I tried to convey a sense of empathy and urgency.

I received a call from our Vice President of Sales, Cindy, about 6 months after joining the company. Her laptop died while she was on the road. I tried to resolve the issue remotely, but could not fix the equipment. I quickly configured a replacement laptop for her and overnighted the workstation to her hotel. I didn't think much of the situation. I was just doing my job.

At the time, I was working for a family-owned business. It started with just a few people in the 90s and grew to over 450 employees by the time I joined the organization in 2008. Our CEO, Michael, attempted to get to know every one of the 450 team members. There are only so many hours in the day and I hadn't met Michael or any of the other executives, despite working at the organization for a few months.

This all changed when I received an email from Cindy. She was so impressed with the laptop replacement process that she felt compelled to email Michael and the rest of the executive team. The senior leadership team replied to the thread to thank me for getting Cindy back up and running. The email probably only took a few minutes to write, but the gesture meant the world to me. As I mentioned earlier, just a few months earlier I had been wondering whether I belonged in the tech industry. I finally realized that I was exactly where I was supposed to be.

I often try to remind myself of the email that Cindy sent. The simple act of letting someone know that you appreciate them and their efforts can have a lasting effect. What might seem insignificant to you might mean the world to someone else.

Go with your gut

I made a friend freshman year at Ohio University named Rob. We lived in the same dormitory and stayed friends throughout college. We ended up staying in touch after graduation as we ended up in similar industries. I was an entry-level IT professional, and Rob was an IT recruiter.

In 2010, I was promoted to IT Supervisor and led a team responsible for IT infrastructure and technology support. I was assigned a large project to replace our company's phone system and had to increase the size of my team. I wasn't sure where to start, so I gave Rob a call.

Rob had built a solid network of entry-level talent that would jump at the opportunity to gain some practical experience. He sent me a few resumes. I reviewed them and scheduled some initial screenings. I remember being nervous about the interviews, even though I was on the other side of the table for the first time in my career.

We ended up hiring one of the candidates. I felt good about his interview, but not great. He had a great resume and spoke in detail about his experience, but something didn't feel right. Still, I ignored my gut and made the hire.

I don't remember when I thought there was a problem after the candidate started, but I am confident it happened on his first day. I can remember being unable to find him at his desk for hours at a time. When he was at his desk, he was reading a book, despite making no progress on his assigned tasks. Things got worse before they got better.

His second day, he didn't show up to work. I ended up calling him to make sure everything was OK. A few hours later, he let me know that he was experiencing car issues but would be in tomorrow. Something didn't feel right.

He also didn't come to his third day of work. Car issues were again cited as the reason for his absence. His recruiter, Rob, offered to drive him to work the rest of the week, but he declined. There was something preventing him from wanting to perform the job.

I ended up giving Rob a call. Not only was this my first hire, but it was also Rob's first candidate placement. We weren't sure what to do.

We came to the consensus that we had to cut our losses. We both would have to explain to our bosses what happened and be transparent. Rather than deflect blame, we decided that we would own the issue and the resolution.

Rob committed to me he would find a replacement by the end of the business day. We were already under a tight timeline to complete the project. I needed to get a candidate on board as soon as possible. I needed to find the right person and I couldn't afford to make another mistake.

Rob kept his word. He introduced me to a great candidate that had exceptional communication skills and a passion for technology. The only caveat was that the individual didn't have any formal technology experience. I decided it was still worth bringing him in for an interview.

We brought the candidate in for an interview the following day. He conveyed to me during the how hard he would work if given the opportunity. On paper, this candidate was the wrong choice, but I felt he would do a great job. I decided that I was going to trust my gut and make the unconventional hire.

The candidate made up for his lack of technical experience by outworking everyone else around them. His positive attitude was also contagious. I learned my lesson: I had to feel comfortable going with my gut.

Don't leave people waiting

One of my biggest struggles career-wise occurred when I assumed responsibility for my company's technology support team. The team had great attitudes, but they were struggling. They weren't able to keep up with the number of tickets/requests that they received from our coworkers. In short, people were waiting.

Before this promotion, I was just responsible for the IT infrastructure team at my organization. We typically didn't receive more than 3-5 requests per day. This made it straightforward to gauge customer satisfaction. The requests to my new team, the technology support group, came from the entire organization, and we often received hundreds per month. I wasn't sure how to keep a pulse on how the team was doing.

Around that time, I met with our contact center director, Karen, to ask her for advice on how to gauge customer experience for large volumes of transactions. She recommended that we send out a quick survey after each completed request. She felt the survey should be short enough that people would fill it out, but long enough that we could still collect some key data.

We landed on the following questions:

- Was your issue resolved?
- Do you feel like we handled your issue with the correct urgency?

- Would you want to have this technician to assist you again?
- Do you have any additional comments?

The survey was helpful and allowed us to gauge customer satisfaction. However, Karen's best advice had to do with the fact that we often left our customers in the dark too long while we were working on their problem or fulfilling their request. The customer didn't have any visibility into the cause of any potential delays. She told me that when we leave people waiting, they usually assume the worst.

Karen gave me a helpful analogy. She told me a hypothetical story about sitting at the restaurant waiting for food. You naturally get frustrated when it takes longer than you expect for your meal to be served. You're a lot more patient and understanding when the waiter stops by every few minutes to share an updated status and offer some water.

Based on Karen's advice, we adjusted our processes. We realized that we would likely always have a backlog of tickets to work through. We made sure that we communicated with our customers every few days to let them know that we still were tracking their issue/request. We also gave them the opportunity to escalate if needed.

This simple procedure helped us several ways. We could self-prioritize our tickets, which let us limit the amount of Work in Progress (WIP). By doing less, we could do more. After just a few months of following Karen's advice, we could improve both the quality and quantity of our work while continuing to keep a pulse on customer satisfaction.

Keep perspective

On 3/31/2014, I experienced one of the largest IT outages of my career. I remember the specific date because it was just before my birthday and I had plans to hang out with my girlfriend (now wife). Shortly before I got ready to leave for the day, I received a phone call from our IT operations department. One of our store-facing systems was offline.

I've worked in IT for a long time and haven't seen too many situations as urgent as an outage that impacts a retail store. This immediately felt like it would be an all-hands on deck scenario. There weren't many people left in the office. I yelled to my friend Kurt to see if he had seen any alerts or was aware of the issue.

Kurt and I dug through system logs. We were trying to find the root cause of the problem. We quickly found out that critical software was uninstalled from a server. The log message included a technician's name. I gave the tech a call on his cell phone.

The technician ran over to my desk. He was testing a future upgrade. The tech wasn't aware that the testing would impact our production system. He was very upset.

We began troubleshooting how to resolve the issue. We quickly realized that the best course of action was to complete the upgrade. We contacted other impacted teams so we could share our plan. The team all agreed that this was the best way to proceed.

The technician that inadvertently caused the problem was

still fretting about the issue itself. We took a few moments to remind the technician to keep perspective. Although the issue was store facing, it was relatively small in scope and store leadership had already implemented a manual process as a stop-gap.

The only thing wrong at that moment was some families were experiencing a delay while returning their children's clothes. We weren't exactly delaying surgeries or preventing an election. While we were impacting the customer experience and needed to take the situation seriously, there was no reason to panic. We needed to focus on the fix as opposed to worrying about the problem itself.

We eventually fixed the issue by proceeding with the upgrade. I could see the relief on the tech's face after we received confirmation that the testing was successful. We knew that we would need to make some changes to make sure this would not happen again. Until then, we knew that the world would keep spinning.

Just do it

I can recall traveling to South Carolina in March 2020 and wondering aloud why our head of HR, Jenni, was considering stopping all non-essential travel because of COVID-19. I didn't think it was worthwhile. Looking back, I wish I had taken the time to understand how this pandemic would impact not just our business but my friends and family, as well.

The only real action I had taken until that point was to order enough laptops to last us throughout our next fiscal year. I was concerned about potential issues with the supply chain. It didn't seem realistic to me that other issues could reach the U.S.

At one point, our contact center director called me to give me a heads up that people were talking about how quickly we would close an office if an employee were to test positive for COVID. A majority of our organization could be relatively mobile except for our contact center. Until that point, we hadn't tested their technology outside of our building.

I started working with our team to come up with some high-level contingency plans. I wasn't sure when or if we needed to act on them. We ended up aligning on the expectation that we should try to have them completed and validated within three business days.

The team came up with a plan in a short amount of time. It was such an enormous relief to have a solution in place. We realized almost immediately that we had hit a roadblock.

The solution would have a significant cost. The cost seemed worthwhile to me, but it was beyond my purchasing approval.

Jenni had taken over the company's efforts to respond to COVID. People had been asking questions, but nobody seemed to have the answers. Jenni never claimed to have the answers herself, but she pulled together a cross-functional team to make sure we found them.

During our first meeting with the COVID response team, I mentioned the roadblock that my team had encountered. It's important to keep in mind that we hadn't even decided that we would send any employees home. I mentioned out loud to the group we had a solution but didn't know if we should spend the money on buying the software.

Jenni responded to my predicament. "Just do it."

It was the decisiveness that I needed to hear at that moment. I realized that hindsight is always 20/20. I was likely going to make some mistakes. I just needed to go with my gut.

We decided that we would do a "stress test" by requiring that two critical departments work from home the following day. Unless we ran into issues, the rest of the organization would work from home the following Monday. If we were going to fail, we would need to fail fast.

Jenni pulled the organization's key stakeholders into a room for an emergency meeting. She shared our plan and gave everyone the opportunity to raise any concerns. Everyone overwhelmingly agreed that this was the right approach. They also felt fortunate to have their voices heard.

During that meeting, I didn't hear our leadership team mention profits. They just wanted to put our people's safety first. Jenni stated that our priorities, in order, were to focus on employee safety followed by maintaining our current book of business and then to shift our concern to new sales. We realized months later that Jenni had boiled down our entire business continuity plan into a few sentences. Our company went through this entire situation without even opening up our crisis response documentation.

This list of priorities helped us decide where to focus as we attempted to close our offices. We made some changes to our network and sent some employees home. After we validated that our changes were successful, we worked to send the rest of our employees home. By the end of our first week, roughly 95% of our employees could work from home without issue.

I hope that I won't need to respond to another crisis in the workplace anytime soon. However, if I do, I will focus on putting people first, being decisive, and failing fast.

Get back on the horse

One of my favorite interview questions is to ask the candidate about the most difficult technical outage that they've faced. I learn a lot about the individual based on how they describe their response to the situation. The individual sometimes asks me the same question. I always give the same response. The most difficult technical outage I have ever been a part of was when my organization's file server crashed, as discussed earlier.

In short, we changed a core system to improve its reliability. We validated our changes. The system ran without issues for two days straight. Suddenly, the system's backups started to fail. We restarted the server, and it never came back online.

The team and I came into the office at 10 PM to troubleshoot the issue. We worked through the night to mitigate the impact of the problem. We ended up rolling back our changes. After being awake for 36 hours, I went home.

The outage really upset me. The lack of sleep didn't help the situation. I told myself and others that I would need to work my butt off to repair my reputation. I was devastated.

After I slept for a few hours, I woke up to a voicemail from Ben, a coworker of mine. He told me a few things that I needed to hear.

First, Ben didn't think I was basing my perception on reality. People within the organization knew negligence didn't cause the outage. The impact was minimal in scope because of the quick actions of the team. Ben felt that the overwhelming consensus was, "stuff happens, that's awesome those guys stayed overnight at the office to fix it."

Ben didn't want me to become hypersensitive because I incorrectly assumed that people would think I needed to right a wrong that people weren't even thinking about. He said that this mentality ends up causing more issues than the original problem itself. Ben felt that people knew where my heart was and that I had an excellent track record.

The last piece of advice that Ben had was for me to understand my emotions. I needed to think about why I was going through them. By gaining a deeper understanding of my emotions, I could try to channel them into something positive. I still reference this advice often.

This situation reminded me of an experience I had when I was in high school. I had just wrecked our family's vehicle. Nobody was hurt, and the car only suffered superficial damage. My dad made me drive the vehicle home.

I thought at the time that he was just being difficult, but he was trying to teach me a valuable lesson. Sometimes when you fall off the horse, you need to jump right back on.

Give praise in public

Even though my initial responsibilities centered on technology support, one of my earliest mentors and bosses, Jim, encouraged me to assume responsibility for systems administration and information security. His encouragement enabled me to expand my skill set, which allowed for continued advancement in my career.

Two years after I joined this company, Jim promoted me to oversee the entire infrastructure team. Jim promoted me even though I did not have any formal leadership experience and had just graduated from college a few years prior. I was very unprepared, but figured this would be a trial by fire. Looking back, I'm confident that Jim saw something in me I didn't see in myself.

Shortly after he announced my promotion, Jim pulled me aside and told me, "I am going to teach you more about leadership in the next five minutes than you learned in any management course you took in college." Sure enough, he explained several management fundamentals that not only enabled me to be successful at this job, but in my future roles.

One of Jim's key lessons was to "praise in public but don't be afraid to reprimand in private." Throughout your career, you are going to run into situations where you must take full responsibility for one of your team member's mistakes, even though the situation was beyond your control. By not reprimanding the individual in public, you will allow them to save face and rebuild their reputation. That doesn't mean that they can avoid accountability, but that discussion should remain private.

Another lesson shared during that initial meeting was to "share the credit but accept all blame." There are few things more demoralizing than when your boss steals credit for your idea or hard work. I had it happen a few times during my career and I struggled with it. That being said, few things made me work harder than recognizing that my boss fell on the sword for one of my mistakes.

I'm still not sure why Jim took a chance on a first-time people leader, but I'm sure glad he did.

Don't lose data

A lot of mistakes in IT can be forgiven as long as they aren't repeated. The business will usually be willing to tolerate temporary outages if you have solid relationships and continue to make forward progress. There is one exception to this rule. Losing data is always unacceptable.

I can only think of one time where my team lost critical business data. Every time I think of the circumstances behind that situation, I feel sick to my stomach. I don't think that feeling will ever go away.

It was a Saturday afternoon, and I received alerts on my phone about a specific server. I didn't think this server was all that critical, so I didn't think much of the issue. The system was just a landing path for archived data. We didn't even maintain a second copy of the data.

We found out that a hardware failure caused the errors. It turns out we lost multiple storage disks at the same time. We should have caught this error in advance. Our alerting system wasn't functioning properly.

I remember thinking we would need to spend some time rebuilding the server and downloading some archive data. It didn't feel like that big of a deal. I thought it would be as simple as notifying our business partners and moving on. That couldn't have been further from the truth.

We found out shortly after we emailed our business partners that a critical process had been storing data on that server.

There was no time to point fingers. We had to restore this data. I felt sick.

We decided that there would be two parallel efforts. One group needed to try and understand the business impact of the missing data. The other group would work to recover the data. I focused on understanding the impact. I needed to prepare myself for the worst-case scenario.

The good news was that we discovered we had some breathing room. The business process that used that data only ran on a monthly basis. This meant that we had several weeks before we had to have the system back online. I shifted my attention to the data recovery efforts.

After some analysis, the team found a way to recover the data from the particular system. However, this recovery method wasn't our core competency. We couldn't risk anything going wrong. We didn't want to lose access to our only copy of the data.

We ultimately outsourced our data recovery efforts. A local firm specialized in these services. They assured us we would have access to our data in a few days. I finally felt that I could relax.

The 3-2-1 rule of backups is a basic rule of thumb to help maintain data availability. You need to have three copies of your data. These copies need to be on at least two different types of storage media. One of these copies needs to be offsite.

Our team couldn't continue to operate based on assumptions. We decided that we would follow the 3-2-1 rule on every system accessible by the rest of organization. We couldn't take any more chances. We needed to make sure that we never found ourselves in this situation ever again.

Follow the money

Perhaps compliance-based security isn't working. Companies have been getting certified as compliant with a particular standard, only to be victims of a data breach just a few weeks after. Compliance frameworks can often serve as a valuable baseline for security. However, I believe that we should look at them as the floor and not the ceiling.

I realized early in my career that I needed to improve the way I communicated security risks. I took a step back to think about what I was trying to achieve when talking about security. I wanted to be transparent about the risks facing our organization. I also hoped to streamline the communication process which would improve our ability to make effective decisions.

It's difficult to communicate risks associated with information security. The best conversations I've had about information security risk involve tying it back to the organization's finances. I've included an example below of what conversations can be like with members of an organization about data security. I've often felt that I provided inconsistent answers to these questions. Despite best intent, I've also thought my concerns get lost in translation.

Example Security Questions

- **CFO**: How much loss exposure do we have?
- **Treasury Manager**: Do we have enough cyber insurance?
- **CEO**: Are we doing enough to minimize risk?

- **CIO**: Are we spending our IT budget appropriately?

I have found that there are a few universal truths in information security. The first is that risk is equal to multiplying probability and impact. We have used this standard calculation to identify and communicate risks for a long time. I could have tried to use more complicated algorithms, but they likely wouldn't have influenced my decision.

The second universal truth is that everyone understands money. I had struggled for years to provide meaningful metrics about security, but they lacked context. For example, there is no reason an executive would understand the impact of us patching 3,000 security vulnerabilities. I wouldn't have that problem if I tied everything back to money.

I can remember thinking there was an 18% chance that my organization would fall victim to a phishing attack. We calculated this based on the amount of individuals that failed our simulated tests. I assumed that the impact of this attack would be $27 million. This meant that the risk to the organization would be $4.87 million.

I often struggled to justify the cost of a security control to limit the effectiveness of a phishing attack. I could now say that by spending $50,000 on two security controls that we would reduce the impact of the attack to $3 million and the likelihood to 8%. This would in turn reduce the risk of a security attack from $4.87 million to $240,000.

Before implementing security control: 18% (Probability) x $27 million (Impact) = $4.87 million

After implementing security control: 8% (Probability) x $3 million (Impact) = $240,000

It became a much easier conversation to say that by spending $50,000, we might hedge $4.6 million worth of risk.

The numbers included in my estimates were based on industry data. I found that I was much more effective in justifying security spend if I could show some level of return on our investments. Security is much easier to justify than it was in the early 2000s. Even so, it's important not to spend money without factoring in how much impact the controls will have on your organization.

This system isn't perfect. There have been plenty of times where our metrics have been questioned and we haven't received approval to fund a security control. The difference is, I believe we're actually all communicating the same language now that we leverage this framework. Regardless of how technical their role is, everyone understands money.

Keep digging

It was a random Sunday. I saw some alerts on my phone I had never seen before. Something didn't feel right. I tried calling one of our main numbers and it rang disconnected. My heart sank.

Our team sprung to action. We forwarded our lines to a third party answering service. It was a Sunday and our volume was minimal. However, this could not bleed into Monday.

To add insult to injury, our company had just hired a new VP of our call center. They were due to walk into our building for the first time as an employee in less than 18 hours. You only get one first impression. I didn't want this situation to be mine. I wanted to put my best foot forward.

We felt our troubleshooting would be more effective if we all met in the office. I ordered some pizza and picked up a stockpile of caffeinated beverages. All logic pointed to the issue being caused by a particular system. After an hour, we were waiting for the manufacturer to isolate the cause of the problem.

I talked to the team about how we should split up who stays at the office and who goes home to get some rest. We needed some fresh minds for the next day if this issue crept into the evening. We mapped out our plan of action in case this issue looked like it would take hours to resolve instead of minutes.

Most of our team had taken a break to let the manufacturer work the issue. Our Network Engineer, Chuck, kept digging. It felt like a dog and its bone. He wouldn't let go.

Out of nowhere, I heard a wonderful sound.

Someone's desk phone was ringing with a call from the outside! I can't articulate how much joy I felt at that moment. Chuck had isolated the cause of the issue. We had restarted one of the critical systems earlier that day but it hadn't "let go" of a failed session. Chuck found a problem that the system manufacturer had yet to even identify.

Chuck eventually fixed the issue. We circled back with the vendors, business partners, and manufacturers. We had a lot of work to do to ensure that this issue didn't happen again.

I learned a lot from Chuck that day. He didn't shift the blame to a third party. He didn't give up until we figured out a solution to the problem. It was the exact persistence that we needed to resolve the problem.

Create alignment

In 2019, I went to a really great conference. One of the speakers was the first female Thunderbird pilot. She shared a variety of great lessons in her talk, but the one that jumped out the most to me was her story about some unwritten rules in the military. These rules became a code of conduct among the team that they referred to as their "wingman contract".

The conference session made me wonder, what are the unwritten rules among our infrastructure, security & operations teams? Was the team following them? Was I following them?

Typically, after attending a technical conference, I return energized to try out a new concept. There's a running joke that I just ask my teammates if they've looked into blockchain every time I attend a conference. Hearing the pilot, Nicole, speak at the conference energized me in an entirely new way. I wanted to make sure the team was on the same page about our code of conduct.

Around this same time, our department's VP rolled out a series of tenets to our IT department. These were a series of standards we wanted to improve on as a department. The tenets ranged from ensuring secure systems to validating that our applications offered a consistent user experience. Each of these standards would help our organization achieve our corporate goals and became a huge part of our strategy.

Our team's code of conduct didn't tie into our corporate strategy or department's tenets. That being said, we still had to come to a consensus about the way we would operate as a team. We had overcome perception issues and a lack of trust among the team. It felt like a logical next step to create a framework to make sure we don't fall back into that trap.

After lots of deliberation, our team adopted the following rules:

- **Go with our guts**: More is lost by indecision than a wrong decision.
- **No surprises**: We need to make sure that we identify issues before our customers.
- **No problems without solutions**: Don't complain just for the sake of complaining. If you are going to complain about a problem, be willing to be a part of the solution.
- **Eat our own dog food**: We need to create solutions that we feel comfortable using ourselves. If we won't use them, why would the business?
- **Stuff happens**: Own our mistakes and work hard to make sure it never happens again.
- **Scratch and dent the car**: Leverage change management to ensure that leadership is ultimately responsible for any issue.
- **Document or automate**: If you repeat the same process repeatedly, ask why?
- **Tell the truth**: Lying is a deal breaker among the team.
- **Get back on the horse**: Allow our team members to save face after an issue and encourage each other to bounce back.
- **Have empathy**: Let's make sure we take the time to walk a mile in other people's shoes. We are a support organization and we can't function without the individuals that make our company money.

Tell the truth

I was up later than usual because the Cleveland Cavaliers were in the playoffs. Just as I was getting ready for bed, an email from a coworker caught my attention. A few of our servers restarted without explanation. This was not good.

Production outages can be overwhelming. To ensure that I am making the best decisions and acting quickly, I follow the OODA (Observe, Orient, Decide, Act) Loop as many times as necessary. This method was originally developed by United States Air Force Colonel John Boyd for military operations, but has also been leveraged for years in the private sector.

Here's an example of my first cycle through the OODA Loop during this outage.

- **Observe**: We found out from our infrastructure monitoring solution that our servers were restarting.
- **Orient**: Our team identified the cause of the server restarts.
- **Decide**: We realized that we needed to make sure additional servers would not be impacted.
- **Act**: We shut down the system responsible for the server restarts.

I hopped online to help research the problem. We quickly found out that our automated process to install updates was causing the servers to restart. I remembered that a team member was supposed to be installing updates on one system but not **all** of them. I called my coworker to ask him for more information.

My coworker said he only configured the system to patch one server. Something didn't add up. We decided to shut down the system that was responsible for pushing out the updates. We had to stop the bleeding.

Immediately after turning off the system, we noticed that the servers stopped restarting. We needed to shift our efforts to understanding the business impact. Fortunately, it appeared that all of the impacted systems came back online without issue. We sent a notice to our business partners to make sure they were aware of the problem.

I ended up staying up all night babysitting a particular server. I wanted to make sure it didn't reboot in the middle of a critical job. We likely weren't at risk of this server randomly restarting, but we couldn't afford to take any chances. If the job didn't run successfully, we could easily have six figures worth of impact to the organization.

I arrived at the office around 6 AM. Things seemed almost too quiet. Outside of a few minor issues, there wasn't much impact. We dodged a bullet, but our work was just beginning.

We had to figure out what caused this issue. The technician continued to state that he did not cause the issue and something within the software malfunctioned. While this appeared to be unlikely, I couldn't operate on a suspicion. I had to confirm this theory.

I started by asking friends and colleagues if they had ever seen this particular system cause dozens of servers to reboot without explanation. Nobody had ever experienced this type of issue. I had operated that same platform while serving as a systems administrator for another corporation and had never personally encountered this type of problem. I decided to reach out to the vendor for a more concrete explanation.

A representative from the software manufacturer began to analyze our system. My suspicion was correct. The logs indicated that the issue was caused by a misconfiguration by my coworker. The worst part of their analysis was the evidence that my team member tried to purge the logs. Not only did he lie about the cause of the issue, he attempted to cover it up, too.

This was a deal breaker for me. It wasn't the first time this employee had been caught in a blatant lie. In my mind, the outage itself was excusable. Mistakes will happen. The lack of trust was my core concern. The cover up was worse than the crime.

Leading a team involves accepting responsibility for things you truly can't control. People are responsible for their own actions. You can't force a team member to act with integrity, but that doesn't mean you shouldn't expect it.

Find a process that works

I can think of a time in particular where I struggled to manage my team's projects. I was responsible for information security, network engineering, systems administration, telecommunications, and technology support. We worked in a fast-paced environment with frequently changing priorities and deadlines. I set a goal to improve and streamline our project communication and collaboration.

We worked in a department comprised of several agile development teams. From the moment I started this job, I was very impressed with the open communication involved with running an agile team. In the back of my mind, I wondered if I could make that work for the infrastructure & security teams I managed. Our teams already held daily stand-up meetings and worked closely with the development groups. Could we take it a step further?

We ended up attempting to leverage agile for an infrastructure-related project. The goal of the project was to replace the portion of our network that is leveraged by our end-users. Unfortunately, we struggled to leverage agile.

We found that the work didn't always fit into standard delivery time slots and often had to be delivered continuously due to inconsistent maintenance windows, etc. We also found that we had to change the schedule to allow us to focus on daily maintenance and keeping the lights on. Finally, we noticed that attempting iterative delivery of this specific infrastructure project was hindering the user experience and negatively impacting the goals of the project.

We ended up trying other methods of project delivery and communication. These included everything from sending email status updates to holding individual project meetings. We even tried using Microsoft Teams to document status updates. These solutions were good, but we wanted something great.

We just needed a few things:

- Open communication
- Continuous delivery
- Clearly articulated priorities

I reached out to my boss, Alex, who ended up giving some great advice that led me to the Kanban Methodology. I ended up doing some research and found that several infrastructure & operations teams had successfully implemented this form of project flow.

I ended up deciding that it was worthwhile for us to test out Kanban and see if it worked for us. At that point, we had to make a few decisions. Should we have a physical or virtual Kanban board? It made sense for us to use a virtual board, but we still had to decide what product to use. Our organization already had subscriptions to Jira and Office 365, which both offered tools for virtual Kanban boards. However, a member of the team was already using MeisterTask and after exploring the UI, we gave that a shot.

We ended up starting with 5 categories:

- **Backlog**: Tasks that haven't been assigned. I was given some great advice to purge items from this category if

they remain dormant for an extended period. If they're dormant for that long they aren't a priority. An extended backlog of tasks that are never prioritized could turn the board into a source of anxiety.
- **Hold/Blocked**: Tasks that have been assigned but can't be completed. This could be as simple as a task being contingent on the completion of another task.
- **Work in Process (WIP)**: Active tasks. Our goal is to limit the amount of WIP to items that can be attended to immediately.
- **Validate**: Tasks that are being tested.
- **Complete**: Completed tasks. We must take time to recognize these items and celebrate success.

After discussing this with the team, there were a few questions that ended up causing us to make a few adjustments to the process. For example, the team already received a high volume of requests/tasks through our ticketing system. Should all of those flow through Kanban, as well? We decided that only items that would take over three business days will be added to the Kanban board.

The team also discussed who would create items for the Kanban board. It was important that we had a clear sense of priorities and didn't introduce too many cooks in the kitchen. We added an extra category for "brainstorming." This is an area to which anyone on the team could contribute. During our weekly project review meeting, we would discuss all open brainstorming tasks and decide whether they should be added to the backlog.

We planned on communicating the status of our tasks during daily stand up meetings, weekly status meetings, and a monthly retro (short for retrospective). During our retros, we reviewed what went well, what we could have done better, and our next steps. We also held retros for any unplanned downtime.

This process ended up working well for us, even though it didn't fit into a traditional methodology. I think my biggest takeaway was the fact that it's not worth limiting yourself to a particular process if it doesn't work for you and your team. Keep iterating. Keep trying.

Plan for the worst

The company I was working for was getting ready to launch a brand new website. This launch involved using technology that the team was unfamiliar with, and we had encountered several unforeseen issues. In short, we were behind schedule and in danger of missing a critical deadline that had been communicated externally.

Thankfully, a coworker of mine named Paul called attention to the fact that we were at risk of missing our deadline. He wanted us to be transparent. Instead of pressing forward and hoping for the best, Paul asked us to meet and come up with a contingency plan in case we were unable to hit the deadline. During this conversation, we learned that we could make some concessions to reduce some of our workload until after the launch. These changes would ensure that we would meet our target date.

Still, the prospects of missing a deadline and/or cutting corners created tension among the project team. At the first inkling of finger-pointing, Paul immediately squashed it. He didn't dismiss the fact that we all made some mistakes. Paul suggested that we hold a formal "retro" at the conclusion of the project. We couldn't afford to be distracted when time was of the essence.

Fortunately, we launched the website on time. The project team met for a retro at a restaurant a few weeks after the site went live. We discussed what went well and the areas we could improve. I remember walking away from that meeting feeling closer to the team, along with a sense of what I could do better next time.

After this situation, I made it a priority to have a better understanding of how failure would impact all of our team's projects. This allowed us to make better decisions throughout the process. For example, I might be less inclined to take a risk if the project deadline is arbitrary and doesn't have any financial impacts. It's just a matter of planning for the worst, but hoping for the best.

No surprises

I took part in a panel discussion for Ohio University students with several IT leaders and a friend of mine from grad school named Kim. At one point after the panel discussion, I mentioned to Kim that I wished I had received the same advice when I was in their shoes. She responded by saying that we probably had, but were too stubborn to listen.

Kim in particular shared some valuable lessons during the panel discussion. The first was a credo that was adopted among her team. "No surprises" has a multitude of meetings for their team members. They use this saying to make sure that their leadership team is never blindsided by a particular issue or outage. Few things make your boss look more unprepared than finding out from a third party about an issue that occurred within their team. While it's difficult to balance fixing a particular problem while also being sure to share the details, effective communication a key component of crisis/incident management.

As I transitioned into leadership, one of my biggest challenges was to stop performing the actual technical work. This was especially difficult during a system/network outage. I thought I was being helpful when I jumped in to address the problem, but I was creating additional challenges. I eventually realized that my role in those situations was to make sure that my team had the support that they needed and that the organization (including my leadership) was not "surprised."

It's also important to identify issues before your business partners discover them. This could be something as simple as implementing a monitoring solution that focuses on user experience. Customers are a lot more patient and understanding when the issues are brought to their attention with transparency and tact, as opposed to them being the ones to identify the problem. Nobody likes surprises.

The second lesson that Kim shared was not to bring up problems without offering solutions. There are few things more frustrating in the workplace than a team member who consistently complains about a particular issue without demonstrating any ownership or offering a potential solution. Mostly, people within an organization want to do the right thing but face complicated decisions. You'll often find they will genuinely appreciate any feedback that you have, especially if you have an idea for how to improve a particular situation. However, complaining for the sake of complaining doesn't help anyone (including yourself).

Scratch and dent the car

I had just started a new job. My team was talented but had some perception issues. I realized pretty quickly that I would need to enforce some changes. The problems boiled down to a lack of transparency, communication, and quality.

I figured I would take some time before enforcing a few changes. I wanted to avoid rocking the boat. I had hoped to sit back and observe before rushing to any conclusions. Unfortunately, that mentality didn't last long.

A technician made some massive updates to a system in the middle of the workday. It was bad enough that these changes happened during business hours. My biggest concern was that the rest of team did not even know these changes were occurring. I realized at that point that my changes couldn't wait. We needed to implement change management ASAP.

I thought back to some roles that I previously held. I remembered the first time I saw change management rolled out to an IT department. I resisted it at first, but our leadership team put things in perspective for me. It was all about making sure that the team members could scratch and dent the car but not total it.

I figured I would get some resistance from the team. Sure enough, I was right. They felt like it would slow them down. There was concern about it impacting their reputation.

I knew I needed to explain why we were making this change.

I shared the analogy that I heard a few years prior. I wanted to put myself in a position where I could accept blame for all the team's mistakes. I hoped that they would just scratch and dent the car but not total it.

We had a lot of debate about what we would consider an official "change" and what we would not. My guidance was that if there was a likelihood, it would impact more than a few users, we would need to document it as a formal change. I had hoped that if they were in doubt, they would lean to be more conservative in their approach. I wanted to reduce risk and improve quality.

About a week later, we rolled out change management. We followed an existing IT process for pushing out hot fixes to our custom applications. An added benefit was the fact that their existing process sent email notifications to the department about upcoming changes. This would immediately improve our transparency and communication.

Leveraging change management forced our team to ask ourselves if a particular modification was worth it. By slowing down, we ultimately improved our quality. We didn't spend our days fighting fires. We could accomplish more.

One thing I hadn't considered was the fact that a lot of our peers didn't know how the team spent their days. This impacted the team's perception. For example, if someone on the team worked at 2 AM performing network maintenance, how would someone know not to expect them to be at the office first thing in the morning? The email notifications to the department of each upcoming change added visibility into the team's workload and helped improve the perception.

We ended up making this change without looking back. It 100% achieved all of our goals. These goals included improving the team's perception, quality, transparency, and communication.

Fail fast

Our company was growing fast and our employees were starting to spread out geographically. We needed a better way to communicate with individuals who didn't work out of our corporate headquarters. To solve this problem, we started testing out some new video conferencing equipment. This was my first marquee project and I wanted us to solve the problem as soon as possible.

Looking back, we performed the right amount of analysis at the start of the project. We met with consultants. We talked to other companies and tested out their equipment. Eventually, we landed on what we felt was a great solution.

I didn't want to waste any more time. We had a solid design and I was ready to start implementation. I wanted to outfit all of our conference rooms with our newly selected gear. My boss suggested we slow down a bit to ensure that we were making the right decision. He wanted us to build out one room and test our configuration to make sure we felt comfortable.

We oversaw the necessary construction on the first room. The entire process took about a week. It felt like people were chomping at the bit to use the new gear. I couldn't wait to show everything off. The room looked great and the solution felt really polished and intuitive.

When we finally started to use the equipment, I felt really proud. I walked some of my coworkers up to the room to show off the gear. We created the necessary training documentation. Our stakeholders also received one-on-one training on how to use the equipment. I thought we were ready.

We weren't able to perform a true pilot because our entire company had unfettered access to the room. Even though we only changed one room out of roughly 30, it would have to be trial by fire. Everyone was excited to test drive our company's the shiny new toy.

Looking back, I ignored a few hiccups that occurred during the first few weeks of testing. A few video calls required technical assistance due to an audio/video issue. I dismissed the incidents as minor bugs that I felt we would eventually figure out. I was so driven to execute quickly that I put blinders on when it came to the bigger picture. The solution needed to be stable if people were going to use it.

The biggest complaint I got was that people wanted us to have more rooms with the video conferencing equipment. I am a people pleaser at my core and wanted to get this done for everybody. I pushed the team to start to scale the solution and install the technology in all of our conference rooms. This proved to be a mistake.

We oversaw the construction in the rest of the rooms. The equipment was installed shortly thereafter. Eventually, we even completed a reconfiguration of our executive board room. We accomplished our goal. Sort of.

Out of nowhere, we started running into a bunch of issues. The cameras would randomly turn off. Sound would stop working out of nowhere. We even ran into a situation where an executive felt it would be easier to just use their cell phone to conference someone into one of the rooms. I was embarrassed.

I decided to treat this as if it was a production outage. During these circumstances, I follow the OODA (Observe, Orient, Decide, Act) Loop as many times as necessary. (I talk a bit more about the OODA Loop during the chapter titled "Tell the truth.")

Here's an example of my first cycle through the OODA Loop during this situation.

- **Observe**: We received multiple reports that our new video conferencing equipment was failing.
- **Orient**: Our team started to track details about the failures including date/time/cause.
- **Decide**: We realized that we didn't have an adequate plan for maintenance and proactive monitoring.
- **Act**: We automated restarts and firmware upgrades of all equipment. We also implemented a portal/alerting system to notify us of potential failures.

Our changes significantly improved the stability of the system. The preventative maintenance and proactive monitoring fixed our problems. It took a while to fix the perception of the solution but we eventually reached that point. I learned a valuable lesson in the importance of starting small and failing fast.

Tell a good story

I accepted a new leadership role in 2016. It was an exciting time in my career. It felt great to join a company that had recently won a "best places to work" award. That being said, there was a lot of work to do from a technical and personnel perspective, and I was eager to get started.

I began by collecting information from each team member about their primary concerns. Overwhelmingly, they cited a lack of system redundancy, and disaster recovery processes. All of our systems operated out of our primary data center in Ohio, with our backups stored at a nearby colocation facility. We didn't have near enough capacity at the offsite facility to restore our critical systems. This was less than ideal.

Working in IT infrastructure, we often have to strive to have our best work go unnoticed. Our team could have implemented a robust disaster recovery program without anyone knowing it existed. That being said, it was clear we needed to focus on copying our systems and network to a geographically redundant data center.

We researched and tested solutions over the next few months. We felt we landed on a robust solution that would help our organization recover in the event of a serious issue. We felt the solution was pragmatic. We weren't spending unnecessary funds but also weren't cutting corners. Unfortunately, the solution still had a hefty price tag.

I did not understand how to sell this investment to our executive team. Even though we had a formal "project charter" process as a mechanism for this project, I wasn't sure exactly how to present it to the group. I put together a slide deck but didn't feel great about it.

I ended up reaching out to a coworker of mine named Ben. Although Ben worked in a different area of IT, he was always my primary sounding board for anything that was user-facing. Ben reviewed my pitch deck and tore it apart. He told me not to overthink it and just tell a story about how we discovered this problem, talk about our research and then present our solution. Ben felt if I used storytelling effectively, nobody would bat an eyelash at the cost.

Ben also advised me to make the problem personal to the executive team. For example, how would this risk impact **them** if it came to fruition? He ended up advising me to tell a story to the executives about what would happen if we encountered a disaster today and then what it would look like if we implemented our solution.

I ended up completely reworking the slide deck. I started my presentation by discussing a hypothetical disaster involving the destruction of our building and colocation. The "fake" disaster concluded with me calling the executive team to tell them that I was not confident **when** or **if** we could bring our systems back online.

I transitioned to talking about how we identified the problem and shared details about our research process. We talked through different disaster recovery solutions and why we selected a "warm site" using cloud technologies. We also discussed our testing process and why we felt comfortable with the solution.

As Ben predicted, by the time I got to the part of my presentation where I discussed the cost of the solution, nobody questioned the investment. In fact, when asked whether we should execute on this project, one of the founders of our company replied by saying, "We have to."

Monitor perception

I don't remember exactly when I realized that my team had a perception issue. There wasn't a general "aha" moment. There were just general inklings of frustration and discomfort among the team and with our business partners. It became very clear to me I would need to make some changes a few months into my tenure at the organization.

Around that same time, another department leader named Alex scheduled a touch base with me. He wanted to share some feedback about my team. He hadn't encountered a lot of the same issues personally, but had overheard a few conversations about my team that weren't exactly flattering. Alex wasn't my direct supervisor, but still made sure I knew he had my support.

That conversation had to have been uncomfortable for Alex. He just as could have ignored the situation. It wasn't his problem to fix. However, he knew it was the right thing to do.

Alex ended up giving me some helpful advice. Even if the perception wasn't 100% accurate, it was likely based on some level of truth. I needed to work with the team to establish a positive perception. This wouldn't be a simple task.

I made one immediate change. I starting acting as if I was the team's business development manager. Relationships needed to be repaired to help drive the team's perception. We would have more patience and tolerance from our business partners when things went wrong if we had stronger relationships. I had to set the expectation for myself that this wouldn't be an overnight process but was still necessary.

I started attempting to build relationships by collecting feedback. There are always two sides to every story. I needed to make sure I was hearing the other side as often as possible. I scheduled a bunch of reoccurring meetings with the team's key stakeholders.

I noticed that most of our business partners had no problem voicing their concerns. I was surprised to learn that many of them hadn't experienced the issues themselves. They heard the problems from another team.

I realized that I needed to find out why a few of the IT teams drove the negative perception for the entire department. I met with the teams that were most impacted by our issues. I wanted to get their perspective on the situation. After hearing their side of the story, I felt that these teams had every right to be frustrated.

It became apparent that a lot of those issues stemmed from a lack of trust with a few specific employees on our team. Their work often took way too long, and when it was delivered, it was usually incorrect. If I was in my business partner's shoes, I would have been frustrated, too. I had to do a better job of managing their performance.

We also had to stop making so many mistakes. It frustrated our peers when their solutions appeared unstable because of issues caused by our team. The technologies we supported were the foundation of the other teams' platforms. We had to take that responsibility seriously.

As a result of this feedback, we implemented a change management process across our team. We needed to come to a consensus before making any changes to production systems. By being more thoughtful about the changes we were making, we ultimately would increase our chances of success. The process change would ultimately improve the quality of our work.

I got the impression that our team didn't take production issues seriously. We often repeated mistakes that had already impacted us before. If nothing else, we had to make sure we saw our failures as opportunities to improve. We should learn from our mistakes instead of repeating them.

We eventually started holding "retros" for all production issues. These retros were often just informal meetings where we discussed what happened. We made sure that we identified the root cause, what went well, what didn't go so well, and what we would do to make sure that the issue didn't reoccur. These simple conversations went a long way to help to reduce the number of issues we experienced.

Eventually things got to a place where our team had improved our perception. It felt like we were adding a lot of value and were truly a part of the department. I'm still appreciative of Alex for taking the time to help our team through a tough situation.

Push your own car

One of the most stressful moments in my career occurred shortly after I found out my position was being outsourced. I went through a variety of emotions, including anger. I knew I had to make a proactive move, but I wasn't sure how or where to begin. I contacted some friends and family for advice.

I ended up reaching out to my friend's dad, Dhuey. Dhuey was an engineer who had been through a similar transition in his career. We met for lunch at Easy Living Deli. He shared some lessons that were helpful in my job search.

Dhuey said that people are going to be more likely to help you if they see you're already attempting to help yourself. He shared an analogy of a broken-down car. People tend to drive past a car at the side of the road. Those same people are more likely to stop when they see someone attempting to fix or push their own car.

He recommended that I send out a weekly email digest of places I had applied to everyone in my network. This digest would let people know that I was working hard and attempting to push my car. When you're unemployed, it's easy to sit around all day feeling sorry for yourself. Dhuey said this weekly email can help hold you accountable.

It also can help expand your network, as your friends may have contacts at the companies you're researching. The goal of this process is to try to get your resume to the top of the stack. I wasn't aware of how many resumes don't even reach the hiring manager until I had this conversation.

Talking to Dhuey made me realize how much work I had to do to build out my network. I had a lot of friends and family members in the Columbus area, but very few of them worked in technology. I didn't want to find myself in this position ever again. I had to take some time to expand my network before I needed one.

I ended up finding a job a few weeks after our conversation. I was able to use Dhuey's encouragement to show that I was working hard to find a new job. One of my friends who saw me "pushing my own car" vouched for my work ethic and recommended me to their employer. I've been fortunate that I haven't had to use Dhuey's advice since our meeting. However, I feel much more comfortable knowing that I have a process in my back pocket.

Remove bottlenecks

I remember thinking as I took on more responsibility that I needed to become an expert on process efficiency and improvement. I asked for people's advice and read a few books. The advice all seemed to center on one key concept. Find bottlenecks and remove them.

The first process I wanted to evaluate was the process we used when we hired new employees. It was important to us that we put our best foot forward and made a good first impression. We wanted to offer a superior onboarding experience for our new coworkers. Even so, we often ran into issues despite our best intentions.

We ended up analyzing our process and realized that the procurement of our laptops was the bottleneck. We would order the laptops directly from the vendor once we found out about a new hire. This sometimes put us in a situation where when we didn't think we would have equipment ready for a new employee.

To fix this issue, we purchased our laptops in bulk. We went from placing 9-10 small laptop orders per year to two large orders. An added benefit was the fact that we could secure additional discounts based on the size of our purchases. We felt comfortable that we had removed the bottleneck in this process.

As great as it was to enjoy this first win, it felt like we had more to do. I realized that our people were our biggest bottlenecks. I asked myself if I was doing enough to free up our most important resources, our team members. It became clear to me that I wasn't.

I decided to tackle a big problem in this area. One of our team's best technical resources was spending a lot of his time focused on technical support instead of designing and engineering. It turns out the business was contacting him directly for help. They were bypassing our formal processes for escalation.

I ended up reaching out to the impacted business partners. I wasn't sure how to approach this conversation. I decided to just be transparent and explain that we needed to encourage cross training among the team to improve our ability to execute. The business partners completely understood.

I noticed an immediate change in the team member's productivity. The cross training also gave other team members the opportunity to step up. Despite our improvements, we didn't consider our work done. There would always be new opportunities for improvement and additional bottlenecks to remove.

Eat your own dog food

When my great-grandfather, Joe Luck, started selling work boots in 1919, he used a pushcart to get his product to Akron rubber workers. One hundred years later, Lucky Shoes is still owned by my relatives and has almost 20 locations around the state. My Father and Uncle also owned and operated a chain of Stride Rite shoe stores in Columbus from 1983 until 2011. I worked part-time at my family's shoe store while I was in high school and learned more about business in the process than I did in four years of college.

At one point early in my tenure at the family business, I showed up to work wearing a brand of shoes we didn't carry. My dad told me I should wear the brands we were trying to sell. If our customers didn't think our family wore the shoes for sale in our store, why should they? This was my first lesson in the importance of eating your own dog food.

In IT, we are often in situations where we can gain early access to the latest and greatest equipment before the rest of the organization. There can be value in IT testing the newest model laptop or piloting the largest monitor. However, this can easily create a sense of resentment among your internal customers. It would be incredibly frustrating to use a 5-year-old laptop while your peers in IT have a brand-new model.

Also, because of our administrative access, we can often circumvent critical security controls used by the rest of the company. If we aren't willing to follow the same rules, why should our customers? If the rest of the organization finds out that the IT team is taking shortcuts to avoid security controls, this will just increase the likelihood that they will make poor decisions to circumvent the controls.

It's important to try to walk a mile in the shoes of your customers. The simple act of shadowing end users on a regular basis has a tremendous amount of benefits. This may identify pain points that you didn't expect. Plus, if the rest of the organization thinks you don't use the solutions you support, why should they?

Encourage innovation

Many companies let their employees devote a certain amount of time to work on projects that might not pertain to their day-to-day responsibilities. This practice allows team members to flex their creative muscles while providing them with the freedom to work without limits. It has led to several successful products, including Gmail. Following this same model, ShipIt days are a 24 or 48-hour period where employees may create and innovate with few parameters or instructions.

My boss, Alex, announced that our IT department would hold our own ShipIt days. He announced the idea to our entire team at a department meeting. In the days and weeks leading up to the event, Alex shared additional details with the group. These details included a few rules.

Our ShipIt days rules...

- We could work on anything we wanted as long as it is not part of our regular job.
- We could work in our system or work area, but not on items in our current backlog.
- The official clock started on a Thursday at 2 PM.
- We couldn't start creating before 2 PM but we could perform research.
- We had to show what we created or learned by Friday at 4 PM by creating a two-minute video highlighting our work and outcome.
- Not everything will be a success, but often failure teaches us the most.

I wasn't sure if I was going to take part at first. I had a lot of work to catch up on and could have used some time to focus on a few tasks. Some coworkers encouraged me to take part in the event. That left me with a very important decision. What should I create?

About ten months prior, I found myself in a situation where we needed all hands on deck to help solve a production issue. Since the issue occurred on a Sunday afternoon, it took me 45-60 minutes to call everyone and explain the situation while discussing our next steps. I spent my time calling instead of sending emails and text messages because these can be overlooked on a weekend. Afterward, I thought about ways that I could automate that process, but I never had time to devote to solving that problem. I decided this would be my challenge for ShipIt days.

Before joining this company, I wrote Python apps and lengthy PowerShell scripts, but it had been about 2.5-3 years since I had even touched a piece of code. Writing and deploying an app in 36 hours was exciting. However, I wondered if I could get the work done in that short time frame. I ended up partnering up with a friend of mine from the department. It had been about 10-15 years since he had written a line of code. We knew we had our work cut out for us but figured we would start by identifying our application's requirements.

The requirements were straightforward...

- The program should automatically call a list of people and play a brief message for them.
- The message should notify them there is a critical issue and that they would receive a follow-up communication with further details.

- The program should send out a text message & email with information about how to dial-in to a conference bridge.
- The program should be easy and quick to execute.
- The program should send out a tweet when executed.

I had seen blogs about how people have creatively used Amazon Dash buttons to automate tasks. Amazon sells IoT Buttons that can be connected to Amazon Web Services (AWS). This seemed like a fun way to kick off our process. Matt connected the button to AWS and ensured that it could execute my Python script.

A ShipIt days project should celebrate failures. I would have been perfectly content if I gave this a shot and didn't produce a working product. I was happy to just spend some time writing code and solving a problem with technology. Fortunately, thanks to some helpful Python libraries and technical blog posts, we had a working script in just a few hours. After a few additional hours of tweaks, we even had the script executing from AWS after pressing our IoT button! We knew that there were potential improvements to make, but we had solved our initial goal!

We didn't end up filming a video. This is mostly because I had to fit in a few meetings leading up to the final presentation. It also resulted from us making code changes until 15 minutes before the projects were due. The lack of a video left us with a much more exciting yet nerve-wracking opportunity…a live demo.

We hadn't tested the IoT button outside of the IT-area and were nervous about the recent code changes that we had made. We ended up configuring the script to call 16 people that we knew would be in the room during the presentations. When I pressed the button, I braced myself for the fact that the indicator light might turn red and the script wouldn't execute. Sure enough, the light turned green and phones around the room started to ring. My Twitter account even sent out a test message.

This activity didn't have any direct benefit to our organization's bottom line. However, there were several intangible benefits that would be difficult to quantify. The effort to innovate ended up having a trickle effect throughout our department. We may not have been working on business-facing initiatives, but our team members worked with emerging technologies that we eventually ended up leveraging. Even if that weren't the case, the camaraderie built during these few days made the event worthwhile and something for us to repeat.

Use situational leadership

My father-in-law has overseen hundreds of team members over the years. You wouldn't think there would be much synergy between his experience in the agriculture industry and my time working in technology. This couldn't be further from the truth. My father-in-law has taught me a lot over the years, particularly the need to use situational leadership.

He helped me realize that I couldn't just treat all of my team members the same. Everyone is motivated by different values. There isn't a cookie-cutter approach for leading a team. It has to be adjusted for each individual.

Based on my father-in-law's advice, I ended up reading a book by Ken Blanchard about the concept of situational leadership. I scored each team member based on their motivation, their perception among their team and business partners, and whether they were a flight risk. I sent a summary of this scoring system to my boss on a weekly basis. It forced me to keep a pulse on how the team was doing and decide if I needed to make any adjustments. I've included an example of what these reports would look like below.

John Doe

- **Flight Risk**: Low
- **Customer Perception**: Average
- **Team Perception**: Good

- **Motivation**: High
- **Notes**: John Doe is a hard worker but can have a short temper which negatively impacts his perception among his peers.

I am a very visual person. The act of mapping out where and how I needed to help my team members was very helpful. Sometimes, this made it clear to me that the best thing I could do for a certain individual was to get out of their way. In other cases, I had to be more involved in the day-to-day activities of a particular person.

This level of transparency also helped me manage up. I could loop in my boss very early in the process if I needed help to guide a team member. This process was also valuable if I identified a gap in someone's pay. I truly think this early intervention helped us retain a few key employees.

It may seem daunting at first. However, I can't say enough good things about taking the time to leverage situational leadership for your team members. No two people are the same. We shouldn't try to manage them that way.

Find the opportunity

On a Sunday morning, while I was out of town, I received a phone call from a team member. Without going into too much detail, we had experienced a significant outage because of circumstances that were beyond our team's control. My boss was out of town and would be on an airplane for several hours. I didn't know where to start.

My wife, Connie, and I packed up our things and jumped in the car. I started by calling team members within the IT department to ask them to come onsite so we could address the problem. I also asked someone to handle communicating with the business. It was a Sunday, so the downtime only impacted a select few, but we had to ensure that the problem didn't bleed into Monday.

Connie could sense that I was frustrated. She forced me to take a step back and think about the big picture. I needed to fix my attitude by the time I got to the office. She reminded me that there is an opportunity in every challenge. This was a chance for me to step up.

Our team worked on tackling the problem while Connie and I drove back to Columbus. I reminded myself that my attitude was contagious before getting out of the car. I helped the team get organized and then got out of their way as they addressed the issues. I reminded the team we had a lot of eyes on us and this was a chance to show off our talent and commitment. The group had a very positive attitude and solved the problem in a very short amount of time.

We ended up receiving company-wide recognition for our efforts. I remember showing up to work the next day, amazed by how little the outage impacted the company. The team's quick actions saved the company hundreds of thousands of dollars. I am convinced that there was a direct correlation between our attitude and the outcome of the situation.

Create a vision

I like to have my team's performance reviews at a restaurant. The change in scenery creates some separation between the review and a traditional status meeting. The goal for these reviews is to facilitate a dialogue where we can talk about career goals, celebrate accomplishments, and identify areas of improvement. A network engineer, Chuck, that I worked with once gave me very helpful feedback during one of these sessions.

During our performance review at Chuck's favorite Greek restaurant, we focused on the concept of start/stop/continue. We started the conversation by talking about things that the team should start doing, stop doing, and continue doing. Eventually, we focused on areas of improvement for both me and Chuck. Chuck felt that I could do a better job communicating my vision.

I was surprised to hear this feedback from Chuck. The more and more I thought about it, he was right. I was very tactical. I had some solid immediate plans but didn't have consensus on a long-term direction. I needed to correct this.

I didn't want to just create a plan in a vacuum. I wanted to involve the team in the long-term vision. If we all felt like we were a part of it, we would want to see it through. I scheduled a meeting with the team to come up with a roadmap.

We came up with a solid plan for how to modernize our IT infrastructure. It felt great knowing that we were all moving in the same direction. It made my job a lot easier knowing that the team understood how some of our smaller projects made incremental improvements towards the long-term plan. As a leader, you often need to explain "why." It's difficult, if not impossible, to do that without a shared vision.

Build a network

When I was in middle school, my dad took me to an Ohio State University football game. It started pouring on our way to the game. Fortunately, we ended up running into a friend of mine that invited us to wait out the rain at their covered tailgate. Towards the end of the tailgate, as the rain stopped, my Dad shared an important lesson with me...it's not just what you know, it's who you know.

As I mentioned earlier, I graduated from Ohio University during the collapse of Lehman Brothers and struggled to find gainful employment. I wanted to make it "on my own" and refused to ask for help. I applied to hundreds of entry-level jobs without even being granted an interview. I eventually realized that nobody truly makes it on their own in how I envisioned. It truly takes a village for anyone to progress in their career.

It became apparent to me I needed help. I reached out to my friends and family to discuss the fact that I needed to find work after college. My aunt responded by letting me know that her employer was hiring interns to complete a project. I applied to the internship and thanks to my aunt's help, my resume likely made it to the top of the stack.

I eventually was hired as an intern at my aunt's company. I gained valuable experience that I parlayed into a full-time role at a health care company at the conclusion of the internship. If I hadn't been willing to ask my Aunt Cathy for help, I likely would have been unemployed for a significant amount of time despite having a college degree. As my dad said, it's not just what you know, it's who you know.

Don't take it personally

I had just completed teaching my first undergraduate course. The class was an overview of network engineering and covered everything from the OSI model to DNS best practices. Despite a few hurdles, the students all passed the course. I got a sense that a majority of them learned a lot in the process.

Teaching this class forced me out of my comfort zone. I had a longtime fear of public speaking. The reputation of giving weekly lectures helped me overcome my fear. I got a little more comfortable with every lecture. Eventually, speaking in public felt natural.

As someone who struggled academically high school, the successful completion of my first college course as an adjunct professor felt like quite an accomplishment. My confidence was through the roof until a student informed me that they decided against a career in network engineering after taking my class. At first, I was crushed.

This student received an A and was very engaged throughout the course. I assumed this meant that I failed my first attempt at teaching. It was hard not to take this feedback personally. I suddenly began second-guessing the lecture material and lab content. I eventually asked the student more about their decision and was pleasantly surprised by their answer.

It turns out, I actually did the student a service. They stated that they really learned a lot throughout the course. They gained enough information about network engineering to decide that it wasn't something that they wanted to pursue.

It didn't have anything to do with the content of the lectures or the structure of the labs. They simply didn't feel passionate about this aspect of technology.

Looking back, I'm really glad this student found out what they weren't passionate about without endangering their career. I just had to separate my emotions from the situation to fully understand the impact. I will keep this experience in mind as I teach additional courses.

As I help students embark on their careers in IT, I will encourage them to seek internships or job shadowing opportunities. This will help them identify if they are truly following their passion or just attempting to earn a paycheck.

Keep improving

Our systems and applications were unstable and constantly going offline. I was constantly falling on my sword with my business partners. Something had to change. We had to start upgrading our processes to improve our quality and our perception.

We started with a simple downtime tracker. A log entry would be created every time we had an unplanned outage. This would allow us to track the issues themselves and hopefully identify some trends. The act of identifying which outages weren't necessarily preventable vs problems caused by human error helped point us in the right direction. We used lessons learned from this report to focus on making incremental improvements.

Around this time, I had seen other teams take advantage of holding formal "retros" at the conclusion of an iteration. These meetings were meant to improve collaboration among the team by encouraging healthy conflict debate. During the conversations, the teams would answer simple questions like "what did we learn?" or "what went well?"

We started to hold retros after each production outage. We focused on things that may have gone well including our communication or actual outage response. Each meeting was concluded by discussing how we could prevent the outage from reoccurring. We wanted to make sure that we learned from our mistakes.

If it was warranted, we would send out a formal root cause

analysis document to our stakeholders. We wanted them to know we took the situation seriously. We also wanted to convey that we were doing everything we could to prevent a reoccurrence. Our hope was to show that there was a focus on continuous improvement.

We eventually reached the point where we started having retro meetings on a regular basis. We identified areas of improvement that impacted people, process, and technology. We left each meeting with action items for each team member. These items helped make sure that we were always making incremental improvements and adding value to the organization.

Don't walk past a mistake

My grandpa, who previously owned his own retail store, often visited the store owned and operated by his sons in Columbus, Ohio. It wasn't just a chance for him to catch up with family, but an opportunity for him to teach others about the principles that made him successful. My grandpa was meticulous about every detail of the stores. The man never walked past a mistake.

Even the way we organized the shoes in the stockroom was important to him. My grandpa used to pull random shoes out of their spot on the wall to see how the wrapping paper was organized inside the shoebox. If didn't look brand new, he would hand it to me to fix. If the customers knew we were willing to cut corners there, where else would they assume we cut corners?

It's no secret that the pair of shoes you're buying has likely been tried on before. However, if the shoebox is a mess before you try on your new shoes, you lose a bit of confidence in the process. My grandpa felt that we should treat each box as if it was a prized possession, and even the aesthetics of the inside of the shoebox was an important part of the customer experience.

I try to follow this mentality to this day. For example, if we're handing out a laptop to someone on their first day of work, it won't give that employee a lot of confidence in our abilities if stickers from its previous owner still cover the laptop. Even though the aesthetics of the laptop have almost nothing to do with the system's performance, it's important to give our customers a sense that we take pride in everything we do.

I look back on these interactions fondly, even if I didn't at the time. I now understand that my grandpa wouldn't have shared this feedback if he didn't care. He didn't want us to settle or cut corners. I now understand why he couldn't walk past a mistake.

Learn to budget

I had just been promoted as a part of a department reorg. Despite my new responsibilities, I was already feeling pretty comfortable and up for a new challenge. It had always been important to me not to step on the toes of my peers while attempting to get ahead. I found the best method was to ask my boss if there was any work I could take off of their plate.

The reorg had left a gap in the handling of our non-labor budget. My boss had intended to take on this responsibility but was already getting used to his new role. I asked if I could take on the challenge. It ended up being one of the best learning experiences of my career.

I wasn't quite sure where to start. I ended up looking over the budget that was submitted the year before. I compared the numbers against what we had actually spent up until that point. I started tracking any variances so that I would have documentation for the next fiscal year.

The planning wasn't as bad as I had envisioned. I learned the difference between operational and capital expenses. I also understood how to justify some of our upcoming needs based on how they fit into the larger picture of our overall budget. The whole experience made me wish I had paid better attention in finance and accounting classes.

I realized that I needed to apply the 80/20 rule to this situation. I was spending 80% of my time accounting for 20% of our budget. I adjusted my focus to spend more of my time on the items that made up a majority of our spend. A minor error in one of these areas could negatively impact our entire budget.

A few months later, I submitted my first budget. It was very conservative. I had moments of panic after everything was set in stone but eventually realized that I had to let that go. No budget would be perfect.

Our numbers started to roll in throughout my first budget year. We were significantly under budget. I remember feeling great and even bragging about how far under budget we were. I quickly learned that this wasn't necessarily a good thing.

It's not always a good thing to be significantly under budget. In fact, it can actually be looked at more favorably to go slightly over budget than be significantly under. My boss, Alex, explained to me that the money allocated to our department could have been spent somewhere else. This may have meant that we didn't the money on marketing another corporate initiative.

Alex taught me about the concept of the zero-based budget. I went into every year with a clean slate. I treated every expense as if it was brand new. It wasn't entirely necessary from an organizational standpoint, but I acted as if I needed to justify every dollar every year.

This mentality completely changed my perspective on how I justified our investments. I forced myself to picture how each new system or capability fit into the larger picture of our organization. I learned a lot throughout this process, but the most important concept was the understanding of how my company made and spent money.

Extend your team

In 2010, the organization I was working for was in the middle of a large phone system cutover. Our system had reached its maximum capacity. We decided to consolidate systems with our parent company to save costs. We had hundreds of custom call tree configurations for our clients. The conversion effort would be difficult.

Our parent company had selected a third-party contractor to configure the call trees based on our documentation. They provided us with access to the system to test the configurations less than a week before go-live. It was apparent that we were in a bad spot. The call trees didn't come close to matching our documentation. Without intervention, our customers wouldn't be able to reach us on Monday morning. I remember my boss saying that if the configurations were code, they wouldn't even compile.

We came up with a process to work with the contractor to correct the call flows. I would centralize all issues our team reported and provide them to the vendor. The contractor was quickly resolving our issues, and it felt like we were finally making some progress. The testing efforts quickly became the bottleneck.

I was only two years out of college. I completely froze. I didn't know what to do. My boss, Jim, stepped in and came up with a great idea. He solicited volunteers from other areas of the business to test the hundreds of call flows. Even our executive team jumped in to help!

I remember asking Jim if he thought people would be OK with us stealing members of their teams. Jim responded by laughing and saying that we were "borrowing, not stealing." He knew how important this project was. Our business partners were happy to help.

All of our testers volunteered to work through the cutover weekend to help us with final validation before go-live. Their efforts meant the world to me. It was inspiring to see team members drop everything and give up their weekend to help with our project. It felt like one big family.

We made all the corrections in time, and we completed our cutover without any significant issues.

Years later, I needed to follow Jim's advice again. My team had been trying for years to roll out a program where we tested all of our applications for security bugs. Unfortunately, my team was small and didn't have much knowledge about the applications themselves. It felt like we would never build out an effective program.

I ended up reaching out to the manager of our quality assurance team. They were responsible for a group of testers that were validating the applications. The team already knew the ins and outs of each application. They would be effective security testers. They just needed some training.

I eventually collaborated with the manager of the QA team to ensure that we trained them in security testing. This ultimately gave them an alternative career path. It also ensured that the organization met our goal of providing secure applications.

Was I directly responsible for this team? Absolutely not. I didn't feel that they needed to report through my organization because they were fulfilling one of my team's core tenents. Ultimately, by swallowing my pride, we could fulfill a goal that I had left untouched for years.

Do the right thing

Getting promoted to director was a career goal of mine, I wasn't sure where to start and how to shift my mentality. I knew I wanted to reach this point, but didn't have a concrete plan of how I would adjust my approach. I decided it made sense to reach out to someone who had been there before.

I reached out to a peer of mine named Steve who at the time was a director of IT solutions delivery. Steve was respected by his team and business partners. We were peers in the organization but didn't know each other all that well. He had just transitioned from a tactical role to strategic a few years prior. I thought Steve would be a great person to chat with.

I had just hoped that Steve would have a few minutes to grab lunch and share some tips. Instead, he spent a lot of time before our meeting preparing a list of helpful guidance. We had a very great dialogue about his shift from a tactical role to a position that's more strategic. Not only did I learn a lot from our conversation, but I often think about the list that he shared with me.

I think the most important thing I learned from my meeting was to make sure I take the time to mentor and help others. They didn't have to take the time to help me out. He did it because it was the right thing to do.

Here's the list that Steve shared with me during our meeting:

- Remember to delegate: don't be critical to the day-to-day operation.

- Don't be the keeper of information: share it so you aren't dragged into tasks others could handle.
- Set up time just to think about what you want to accomplish and what has to get there.
- When asked to build out a new process or feature, ask yourself if you would do this "thing" if you were setting up a new system or company.
- Always think about business value and longevity of something new.
- If you are doing the same thing every day, question it.
- Involve others in an idea so they can help champion it.
- Don't force things on the business - listen and see how you can achieve both their goal and yours.
- Look for ways to get new perspectives - move people around to stretch them and challenge the status quo.
- Ask lots of questions - throw out stupid ideas. Be curious about everything.
- Find someone who disagrees with you and get their perspective.

Measure it

"If you can't measure it, you can't improve it."

Those words went through my head after I was promoted to a new leadership role. As I stepped away from the day-to-day responsibilities for my teams, how would I measure their success? How would we show our success to our business partners?

I had purposely avoided metrics in the past. I had concerns that team members could gamify the statistics to appear more successful than they really were. I also wondered if my business partners and peers would really care about these metrics. Despite my reservations, this still felt like a worthwhile endeavor.

Every group is unique. The goals that worked for my teams at that may not be effective for others. In fact, they didn't even translate well to other disciplines in our department. They still worked well for us.

Around this time, my coworker introduced me to the concept of the "North Star Metric". This just meant making sure that one of your metrics sums up the value of your team or platform. We picked system availability as our North Star Metric. Our jobs as IT infrastructure professionals centered around creating the foundation used to run our software solutions.

The act of collecting these metrics took some time. The time ended up being worthwhile as the statistics helped us keep a pulse on our effectiveness. They also served as a way for us to show our value to our business partners.

Here are the metrics we leveraged...

- **Mean Time to Detect (MTTD) outage**: This statistic will show the success of our monitoring program. It was important that we identify issues before our business partners noticed them.
- **Time to Restore Disaster Recovery (DR) Environment**: Keeping a pulse on this metric will ensure that we are continuing to improve our organization's ability to recover from a disaster. It will also show how often we are testing our DR processes.
- **DR Recovery Point Objective (RPO)**: This will help us paint a clear picture to the business of how much data we would likely lose in the event of a disaster.
- **Website Availability**: We selected this metric because at the time, our website was hosted out of our data center. We had to take the website offline every time we performed network maintenance. This helped us show the ROI for a cloud migration effort.
- **Phone System Availability**: Our phone system was also hosted out of our data center at the time that we started to collect these stats. We used the improvement of this metric to justify consolidating platforms and moving to the cloud.
- **Tech Support Survey Results**: We asked some basic questions in an automated survey after each help desk ticket was closed. The results helped us keep a pulse on the customer experience.
- **Code Releases Per Month**: As our teams moved towards a Continuous Integration/Continuous Delivery

model, this metric would help us demonstrate progress in this area.
- **Percentage of Server and Application Configurations Automated**: This statistic helped us show how much progress we made automating the deployment of our infrastructure.
- **NIST Compliance**: We used this to quickly explain to leadership how compliant we were with industry security standards.

Find a cause

After finishing grad school, I had a strong urge to volunteer. I wanted to make an impact. Unfortunately, I didn't quite know how to devote my time. Should I go to a soup kitchen? Meals on wheels? I reached out to a coworker of mine named Jen and she gave me some wonderful advice. She told me to find a problem I was passionate about fixing. The more and more I thought about it, the unnecessary barriers that were preventing talented individuals from entering the IT workforce frustrated me.

I was fortunate enough to have an opportunity to invest time and money into receiving a formal education at Ohio University. My formal education served as a great way to show my work ethic and desire to learn. It ultimately got my foot in the door of a great company and helped kick-start my career. In my mind, there had to be a way to help less fortunate individuals show those same capabilities while gaining some practical experience.

I learned more about business working at our family-owned shoe store in high school than I did receiving a minor in business administration. Rather than sit back and complain, I tried to fix the problem from the inside. I started teaching classes at Franklin University. As much as I loved helping the students, it wasn't enough. I wanted to do more to remove the barrier preventing talented individuals from entering the IT workforce.

Fast forward a few months and my coworker introduced me to a nonprofit founder. The founder spoke to us about a program that had started in Chicago called i.c.stars. The program identifies, trains, and jump-starts technology careers for low-income young adults who, although lacking access to education and employment, show extraordinary potential for success in the business world and likelihood to make an impact in their communities. Candidates who enroll in i.c.stars immerse themselves in the program. They go through a four-month training cycle and spend 60+ hours a week working on real projects for organizations.

The numbers from the original office in Chicago spoke for themselves:

- 300+ total alumni
- 95% initial placement rate
- $9,915 average annual earnings before the program
- $57,240 average annual earnings 30 months after program completion

Even after seeing those statistics, I was skeptical. I didn't think that i.c.stars could prepare individuals with little-to-no technical experience for a career as a business analyst, project manager, QA analyst or developer in four short months while also delivering a working product. My company served as the first project sponsor for i.c.stars Columbus. We saw a partnership with i.c.stars as an opportunity to give back to our community and change lives for the better.

They split the group into several teams that worked to build us a dashboard to display information about our system transactions. I can definitively say after serving as the organization's first project sponsor, I had no reason to be skeptical. I am still amazed by the growth that I witnessed during the initial four-month program.

The i.c.stars alumni found jobs all over Columbus after the program was over. We even hired a former student at my employer. Their success in the industry led me to reconsider my own hiring practices. I needed to practice what I was preaching.

This started with just removing degree requirements from job descriptions but evolved to hiring individuals without formal technology experience or education. I've seen these efforts adopted by others at my company. I hope that other companies will consider helping talented individuals get their foot in the door.

I can think of a few times throughout my career where I took the easy way out in terms of hiring. We ended up bringing on a more seasoned professional because it was the safe move. Looking back, I wish I had prioritized giving someone a chance to enter the technology workforce. Yes, an entry-level candidate will require more training which can slow your team down. Yes, it will take a while before someone with limited experience can make meaningful contributions. That doesn't mean that they're not the best candidate for the role. Sometimes, it's a matter of just doing the right thing.

Learn by observation

I was part of a small group of IT professionals who attended a presentation by/conversation with Major League Baseball Coach, Terry Francona. Terry geared a lot of his conversation towards his approach to leadership. One of the key concepts that initially jumped out to me was the fact that he tries to create a culture where the team "wants to come to the ballpark every day and do the right thing".

When I first became a hiring manager, I focused too much on technical aptitude during the interview process. I asked detailed questions about a particular system or network, but didn't spend much time talking about how they approached situations or problems. While we ended up hiring team members that had a lot of valuable experience, they sometimes they lacked a genuine passion for technology. In more extreme instances, they didn't work well with other team members. I needed to make some adjustments.

Since hearing Coach Francona speak, I've focused more on hiring the qualities that can't be easily coached or developed. This has led me to work on finding individuals interesting in learning about how the technology works, as opposed to just technicians who have gathered massive amounts of knowledge. I also try to gauge whether the candidate operates with a high level of integrity. These adjustments have helped create a culture where all of our team members want to come to work every day and do the right thing for our customers.

Another lesson I picked up on during this talk was to learn by observation. Terry Francona mentioned a lot of the managers he coached with and played for during his career. He said that he learned a lot about how to be a coach by playing for great coaches. You might never get the chance to sit down and have a career-focused conversation with someone that you admire. Fortunately, there is ample opportunity to learn from the example that they set and how they approach a particular situation.

Through observation, you can also learn valuable lessons about what not to do. This part of the conversation reminded me of times in my career where I worked for less than stellar bosses. I took the time to think about what they did in particular that I found demoralizing. It made me realize that I need to consider not only what motivates a team but what could demotivate them.

The first thing that came to mind was when a boss of mine took credit for an issue that I resolved. Our employees could not access their email. The technical team couldn't figure out what was causing the problem. I suggested restarting a server that hadn't been reviewed as a part of our troubleshooting process. My boss ended up performing the actual restart. When our CIO stopped by to ask about for more details, my boss took full credit for the fix without mentioning that it was my original suggestion.

I ended up reflecting on similar moments in my career so I could better understand behaviors to avoid. I didn't want to demoralize my team. I had learned a lot about what my previous bosses did well. This talk made me realize I could learn just as much from where my old bosses missed the mark.

I had hoped to just shake the hand of a future Major League Baseball Hall of Fame member, but I walked away with some lessons in leadership that will hopefully serve me well for the rest of my career.

If you want applause, join the circus

I hit a point early in my career where I became disgruntled. I felt I could make much more money working for another company. I also didn't think my then-employer appreciated my work. Looking back, it wasn't just the lack of pay and recognition. I was unhappy with the role itself.

I vented to my dad about my circumstances. He assured me that if I kept my head down and worked hard, eventually someone would notice and recognize my efforts. My dad told me that if I wanted applause, then I should join the circus.

I've kept this in mind throughout my career. It's particularly worth considering when you specialize in IT infrastructure and operations. In these areas of IT, you often need to make sure that your best work goes unnoticed. For example, a network upgrade that takes months of planning and analysis should be transparent to the end-user.

The organization doesn't always think to recognize a team or individual when systems work as expected. This may unfortunately create a situation where certain teams only hear from their peers when things go wrong. It's not intentional by any means. Familiarity breeds contempt, and people inadvertently take things for granted.

It's important to note that the higher that you climb the corporate ladder, the less recognition you'll receive yourself. Your goal should be to make sure your team is ultimately recognized for the group's successes, not you. If you thrive on validation, you may need to adjust your expectations. Your team's success is your success.

Turn friends into family

Anthony was a very skilled member of our technology support team. He joined our department after working for a few years in another area of the business. Anthony immediately hit the ground running and became a really positive part of our team's culture.

I received a notification on my phone from a coworker named Anthony one Sunday that scared the heck out of me. Anthony's message asked if anyone could cover his on-call shift because of a house fire. He assured us everyone was OK, but he needed to be away from his phone for a bit. I covered his shift and didn't think much of it. Anthony was so calm in the way he approached the situation, I assumed the fire was small in scale.

Then he sent a video of his house. The fire destroyed almost everything. His family was lucky to have survived. I, along with others on the team, asked if there was anything we could do to help. Anthony's attitude was so positive and uplifting. He referred to it as a "transition."

We had a mechanism in place called the hardship fund for situations liked this. The IT and HR teams immediately linked Anthony up with the group responsible for the fund. It was great that everyone responded so quickly, but it didn't feel like we had done enough.

A few of Anthony's coworkers created a GoFundMe to help

his family get back on their feet. Their initial goal was to raise $1,000. The link kept getting passed from department to department. Everyone wanted to help Anthony. The fundraiser cleared over $8,500 in a matter of days!

This situation reinforced that there are more important things than work. Our team didn't want to look back on this moment and wish we had done more for Anthony. I was inspired by how quickly Anthony's friends and coworkers jumped into action to help him get back on his feet. This spoke volumes to our people-first culture. It also highlighted Anthony's unique ability to turn his coworkers into friends and his friends into family.

If it hurts, do it more often

Every company has a system or application that the whole IT department is afraid to touch. It could be a legacy system a former colleague created. The application could be critical to the company, but still very fragile. I have dealt with my share of these systems over the years.

I recall one system in particular when I think about something that was fragile yet critical. Our team was performing some maintenance on a system. Ironically, we were trying to add redundancies that would improve the system's reliability. On a few separate occasions, we tried to make these changes and ultimately had to revert them. It just seemed like every time we touched the application, something broke.

After one particularly grueling problem, we got everything fixed. We had to make a bunch of manual changes to correct the issue, but ultimately everything was back up and running. It felt like the right move was to just leave the system as-is. Deep down, we knew that we had more work to do.

We needed to rebuild this system so that everything could be configured automatically. This would mean that we wouldn't need to rely on our team's institutional knowledge to change the system. The code and automation itself should be the only documentation that we would need. We couldn't afford to have any more "skeletons in the closet."

Our team ultimately pushed to move down this path. Our

motto quickly became "if it hurts, do it more often." We realized that the longer we went on in a state where we had fragile systems, the worse we would ultimately be. Even if it meant that we would need to deal with a certain level of risk in making these changes, we needed to pursue them.

Ask the right questions

I had just taken over as a product manager for one of our application development teams. I had a lot of strong relationships on the business side. I even understood the line of business and how some of their systems tied together. I knew nothing about software engineering.

Part of my role as a product manager involved approving emergency changes to our systems. I needed to lean on the application development team to justify why the change needed to be made outside of our standard maintenance window. The typical rule of thumb was that we should leverage an emergency change in situations where we couldn't wait until our standard window to fix an issue. Performing a hot fix can be like changing out the engine of a moving car.

Within my first few weeks, I ended up approving a change request. I didn't think much of it. If I recall correctly, the alert popped up while I was in a meeting. I pulled out the virtual rubber stamp and moved on.

A few hours later, I saw that our technology support team received a spike in calls about a system failure. I wondered if it resulted from the change that I had approved. I felt sick. Why didn't I take a few extra minutes to make sure I understood the impact of the change? Why didn't I ask more questions?

It turns out that the issue was a complete coincidence. It had nothing to do with the change that I had approved. It didn't matter. I had already learned my lesson. I needed to ask more questions.

I had followed this process while managing the IT infrastructure team for years. I wasn't concerned about approving these changes because I had a solid understanding of how those changes could have impacted the business. It was a lot easier because I had served in most of the different roles on the infrastructure team over the years. I didn't have this luxury with our application development team.

I realized that this needed to be a core part of my approach for helping to lead this team. I accepted the fact that I would sometimes need to ask questions that may be obvious to the rest of the team. This approach would ensure that I heard all the facts before calling the play. Sometimes, effective leadership seems to be a matter of asking the right questions.

Focus on your industry

When I was ready to graduate from Ohio University in the summer of 2008, I knew I would start my full-time internship at a hospital immediately following graduation. My degree had focused on theory. My lack of technical skills concerned me. I debated which technical certificate to study for in the few months before I started at my internship. I knew I had to learn something, but I couldn't quite figure out what.

My professor asked a few questions related to my predicament. His advice was for me to spend my time learning about health care and hospitals as opposed to just focusing on technology. Their advice still holds true today. Technology constantly changes. By focusing on your industry, you can help build practical solutions and serve as a business partner as opposed to being a technologist.

When I think about the most valuable employees I have worked with, they often have the most institutional knowledge about our company and industry. This has enabled them to embrace technical change while still keeping a focus on the organization's mission and vision.

Since stepping into a leadership role, I have found it overwhelming to see the technology I used to support rapidly change before my eyes. I've deliberately chosen to keep my knowledge of these changes at the surface level and focus on expanding my knowledge about our organization and the energy industry. I hope that this will help empower team members to focus on technology execution while I work to set the tone for our overall strategy.

Recognize others

I wrote earlier about a time I saw Terry Francona speak. He is a manager of the Cleveland Indians and a personal hero of mine. During his speech, I learned several great methods for building camaraderie within a team. One of the best methods was his "spring training award."

During his speech, Terry Francona talked about an award he created when he noticed his team was in a funk. He asked a player to recognize another member of the team by giving them an award after each spring training game. They required the award winner to hold on to the award until the next game when they passed it on to another player. He noticed that the act of the team celebrating each other's accomplishments helped to build camaraderie among the team.

I decided this was something that I wanted to replicate with my group. I went to the trophy store and purchased the strangest looking one that I could find. If I recall correctly, it was a trophy made to look like a giant turkey. We called it the "garbage award" which was meant to be a term of endearment among the group.

We held weekly team meetings where we would review our work in progress and items that met our definition of done. I gave out the award for the first time to an employee that had gone above and beyond during the prior week. I requested that the first recipient hold on to it until our next meeting. They passed it on to another member of the team who stepped up during the time between our gatherings. This process continued for years.

Do the dirty work

While working at the family shoe store growing up, I learned a lot about the concept of servant leadership by observation. My dad would take out the trash and unload shoe shipments. My uncle would work as a salesman during the busy season. They wanted their team to recognize that the work wasn't beneath them.

The decision to join a company after an interview feels like getting married after one date. You can ask all the right questions and still miss out on a key detail that will make your job experience miserable.

On my second day of work at a new job, my boss that went on a bit of a rant about how he wouldn't be helping us out much because he had already paid his dues. He told us he had been in an on-call rotation for a decade and wouldn't be taking part in our rotation. My boss wasn't even willing to cover a few hours at a time so we could spend uninterrupted time with our families. This attitude killed my motivation.

I took part in the team's on-call rotation when I became a supervisor for the first time. I wanted to show the team I was in it with them. I didn't want them to think I felt certain tasks were beneath me. I also wanted to get a better understanding about how my decisions impacted the team.

Eventually it got to a point where my role was far enough removed from execution that I wasn't able to offer much help during evening/weekend maintenance. However, I tried to at least log on to the conference bridge to show my support. It's tough to find the balance between helping and getting in the way, but when in doubt, I tried to at least show that I cared.

You break it, you buy it

A network engineer named Wes that I've worked with over the years has helped build up a lot of green team members throughout his career. Wes has a unique ability to own the responsibility of their project work while ensuring they get all of the credit. He has one steadfast rule while encouraging them to find a balance between risk and reward when it comes to a technical change. His main rule...you break it, you buy it.

What Wes is articulating with his rule is the need to instill a sense of ownership at the point where a team member's technical training wheels are removed. This can help give a level of assurance to someone uncomfortable with a particular change or project. If you're the one to take a chance without supervision, you're the one responsible for owning that change and ultimately finding the resolution. If you don't feel comfortable, make sure you get some help.

Even as I stepped away from day-to-day technical responsibilities, Wes maintained their "you break it, you buy it" rule for me. I needed to own the work I was completing as opposed to just hoping that someone would ultimately clean up my mess if I had to step away to focus on my leadership duties. It caused me to take a step back, focus on providing strategic leadership as opposed to interfering with ongoing technical work.

Wes' rule has helped individuals transitioning to careers in IT build confidence and make immediate contributions. I still leverage this mindset daily and will into the future.

Know when to move on

When I first started my career in IT, my friend's dad introduced me his CIO, Larry. Larry and I immediately clicked, and he served as a great mentor throughout my career. We always met up for lunch at the same breakfast place. I could tell he really enjoyed helping me, even as some situations became very difficult to navigate.

One situation that Larry helped me through was when I was working at an organization and had been passed over for a few promotions. I can say now that as I reflect on the situation that it wasn't that I wasn't the right fit for those roles, but I wasn't fulfilled by what I was doing. The culture was bringing out the worst in me. I just wasn't happy.

Larry told me that it's important to know when to move on. Chances are if I had been passed over a few times for new opportunities that I would likely need to make some serious changes or consider looking for a new employer. Something wasn't working. I needed to be more introspective and find out why.

Ultimately, I took his advice and ended up starting looking for a new job. I was concerned that my resume would reflect a lack of loyalty because I had moved around a few times in a short amount of time. I needed to make sure I landed in the right spot.

This analysis helped me create a framework for identifying a good employer. If I look for a change in employment, I make sure I feel comfortable answering the following questions.

It's a very serious decision and worth taking extra care to make sure you make the right choice. Accepting a job offer sometimes feels like getting married after 2-3 dates. It's worthwhile to exercise caution.

Questions to ask yourself...

- Is the industry ripe for disruption?
- How is the organization doing financially?
- Do I know anyone who works there? How do they speak of the company's culture?
- Why is the role open? Is it a new position or was it recently vacated? If someone recently left, why?

Play chess, not checkers

Information security can be frustrating. You're always going to find yourself in positions where you have to make pragmatic compromises. New business features are often more important than fixing security bugs. I can think of one particular instance where this decision frustrated me.

I sat in on a meeting about fixing a security issue in an in-house built application. We were told that we wouldn't be able to fix the bug anytime soon. My team and I were furious. This wasn't a trivial amount of work, but the vulnerability was easily exploitable.

I took a step back to think about the situation. I realized it wasn't worth getting mad. We had a process in place to escalate security issues. We reviewed all of our risks with senior IT leadership on a regular basis. They either had to accept the risk or allow us to prioritize putting a fix in place.

Because leadership had to acknowledge every bug in our systems, the problem we identified would eventually surface. I had a feeling that our CIO would refuse to allow this bug to survive. It was too risky.

As expected, they refused to sign off. We instructed the team to fix the bug as soon as possible. We ultimately got the same result we had hoped for. It wasn't worth getting upset. I realized that sometimes it's just a matter of playing the long game.

Be a duck

At one point, my company's CTO, Brandon, pulled me aside to let me know that he would invite me to a meeting later that afternoon. This meeting would be the kickoff of an enormous project that would impact every employee in the organization. It was abundantly clear to me that the IT team would play a large role. I was freaking out.

I've been told that I have the world's worst poker face. It must have been abundantly clear that I was already panicking about the upcoming endeavor. I knew it would be a lot of work in a short amount of time. Brandon easily sensed my discomfort and advised me to "be a duck."

I did not understand what he was talking about. Why should I pretend to be a duck? Brandon explained that a duck may seem calm, but underneath the surface, they're doing everything possible to tread water. They inadvertently project a sense of calm even though they're struggling to keep their head above water.

I realized why I needed to project a sense of calm to the IT team members and the rest of the organization. As a leader, my actions and attitude can be contagious. If I appeared panicked or stressed, it could spread to the rest of my team and perhaps others in the company. This conversation with Brandon made me realize that I was worrying about things that either won't happen or were beyond my control. Instead of wasting time getting worked up, I realized that I needed to take a step back by beginning to understand the project and working with my coworkers to solve the problems.

Over the next few months, we put together comprehensive plans for the project. I immediately felt at ease as we broke down the work into digestible chunks. Once we executed on our strategy, I felt even better about our ability to meet the aggressive timelines. At one point, I wondered why I ever got so worried.

When in doubt, be a duck.

Summary

For the CliffsNotes fans, here's a summary of the lessons from each chapter…

- Take the time to celebrate success and recognize others.
- Working in IT can be stressful. This is especially true when you are helping your team through an outage. Make sure you keep perspective.
- During stressful times, make sure to project a sense of calm. Your attitude is contagious.
- Just showing up is half the battle. Your team members will appreciate simple gestures more than you will ever know.
- It's OK to sweat the small stuff. A lack of attention to detail reflects a lot on you and your team. Make sure your team takes pride in the little things.
- Help your team find the opportunity in every challenge.
- If you find yourself in a crisis, begin by putting people first. You'll find yourself making a lot of huge decisions. Try to break them up into small decisions and be decisive. Finally, set yourself up so that if you fail, you do it quickly.
- Give praise in public but reprimand in private.
- Don't force solutions on the organization that you wouldn't be willing to use yourself.
- Don't wait until you need a network to create one.
- Technology will always change. Focus on learning your employer's industry and how your company makes money.

- People will be much more likely to help you if they see you helping yourself.
- Don't be afraid to ask for help. Other departments are often willing to help your team reach their goal.
- Own your mistakes and make sure that you're the one to fix any problems that you create. Also, trust your gut.
- Instill a mindset of accountability across your team.
- Be prepared for tough conversations.
- Keep a pulse on the perception of your team.
- Put your team into a position where you can be 100% accountable for their mistakes.
- Take the time to make sure your boss and your business partners aren't surprised.
- Make sure you have a plan B.
- You won't always have the opportunity to sit down and chat about leadership with people that you admire. However, you can learn just as much by observation.
- Just because a process worked for someone else doesn't mean it will work for you. Keep adjusting and improving.
- Create a culture that supports innovation.
- Make sure that your team conducts themselves in a way that supports each other and the goals of the organization.
- Help others even if you don't get anything back in return.
- Your team should celebrate success among each other.
- Whether you realize it or not, IT leaders are in sales. Storytelling is an important way to get others to buy into your proposed solution.
- Constantly communicate. The longer people go without hearing from you, the more they tend to assume the worst.

- It's not always the obvious solution. Keep digging.
- You can adopt all of the latest Scrum methodologies and have the most expensive tech but you can't accomplish anything without a great team.
- Don't be afraid of any system or process. Either document it or modify it until you feel comfortable.
- Don't fake it until you make it. Ask the right questions until you feel comfortable.
- No two people are the same. Don't try to manage them that way.
- Give back to your community.
- You and your team are going to make mistakes. Do what you need to do rebuild your level of confidence.
- A leader without followers is just a guy taking a walk. Collaborate with your team on a vision and follow it together.
- You may not be in the right place. Sometimes, you need to know when to move on.

"Virginia Tech - data center" by cbowns and "Data Center Frosinone 2" by seeweb are both licensed with CC BY-SA 2.0.

About the author

Since receiving a master's degree from Ohio University, Adam Luck has overseen the implementation of IT infrastructure and information security solutions for organizations ranging from small credit unions to Fortune 500 companies. He is an IT director for IGS Energy in Dublin, Ohio, where he leads a department of 30 individuals with responsibilities including information security, dev ops, network engineering, systems administration, database administration, telecommunications and technology support. Adam also serves as a product manager by setting direction for a cross-functional team comprising developers, quality assurance testers and business analysts responsible for software solutions designed to support the organization's home warranty business.

Adam is passionate about improving technology education. He has channeled this passion by serving as an Adjunct Professor in the Computer Science department at Franklin University since 2016. At Franklin University, he teaches courses that cover network engineering, systems administration & information security. He also volunteers as an advisory board member for technology programs at Ohio University, Hocking College and Tiffin University. In his role as advisory board member, he works with University administration and faculty to help align the school's curriculum with the needs of prospective employers.

He is also committed to improving the communities where he works and lives. To continue this commitment, he has accepted a role as a member of the board of trustees at Alvis,

Inc. Alvis is a nonprofit human services agency with 50 years of experience providing highly effective treatment programs. Their lines of service include research-based, comprehensive reentry and family support programs; behavioral health and substance abuse treatment services; recovery housing for women and their children; and services to individuals with developmental disabilities who are trying to live more independently in the community. As a member of the board of trustees, he acts as an ambassador for the organization, helps make governing decisions, and helps secure the resources and financial support to advance the Alvis mission.

Adam lives in Columbus, Ohio with his wife, Connie, and their dog, Newman.

www.ingramcontent.com/pod-product-compliance
Lightning Source LLC
Chambersburg PA
CBHW071411210526
45465CB00001B/335